Birds + Bees + *YOUR* Kids

A guide to sharing your beliefs about sexuality, love, and relationships

Amy Lang, MA

Birds + Bees + Kids®LLC
birdsandbeesandkids.com
206-661-2245

Design: Christine Marie Larsen / ChristineLarsen.com

ISBN: 978-1-59849-091-6

Printed in the USA

Peanut Butter Publishing
2925 Fairview Avenue East
Seattle, Washington 98102
877-728-8837
www.peanutbutterpublishing.com

Table of Contents

MY STORY

Thanks so much for purchasing this guidebook. I know how hard it can be to talk about sexuality, love, and relationships with your kids. Even though I talk about sexuality for a living, sometimes I am still uncomfortable talking to my son. Whether your kids are 2 or 22, my hope is that once you complete this guide, you will feel encouraged and inspired to start and continue conversations with your kids all through their lives.

Throughout my 20's and 30's I provided sexual health education, primarily as a volunteer, for several non-profit organizations in the Seattle area. I worked directly with patients and provided counseling about pregnancy, birth control, sexually transmitted infections, and HIV. I discovered that I love talking about sexuality, and in particular, those aspects of sexuality that are more challenging or difficult.

However, when my son had questions about his body and its workings, I was surprised to discover that I was uncomfortable talking to him! I started thinking and realized that if I was uncomfortable talking to my child, other parents must be even more uncomfortable. Spurred on by my own discomfort, I decided to start Birds + Bees + Kids® to help parents become informed, confident, and comfortable talking to their children of any age about sexuality, love, and relationships. I provide parents and caregivers with an environment that encourages them to explore their personal values about this topic and then decide what is right for their family based on their values.

I live in Seattle and have been married since 1993. We have a young son who keeps us on our toes, playing Legos, digging, and asking questions like "How long do you have to lie like that?" when we talk about how babies are made.

Feel free to contact me if you have questions, concerns, or would like to schedule a workshop, talk, or phone consultation. I'm happy to help!

Birds + Bees + Kids® LLC
birdsandbeesandkids.com
amy@birdsandbeesandkids.com
206-661-2245

This guide will feel very much like a personal, private journal and take you through the process of articulating your values around sexuality, love, and relationships.

- It will ask you questions and prompt you to respond in writing. Go ahead and write in the book – that is what it is meant for.

- The process, if done in one sitting, should take about 2 hours.

- Do it in private or with a caregiver partner.

- At the end, you will have a complete document that provides clarity for you around your values. You can refer to it as you have conversations with your kids as they grow.

- Resources are listed in the back.

Chapter 1

SEXUAL VALUES—WHAT ARE YOURS?

SEXUAL VALUES—WHAT ARE YOURS?

You know you need to talk to your kids about sex at some point—every parent knows this, right? But where on earth do you start? And how old should your kids be? What if they say they already know everything and won't talk to you at all? What if they ask you how old you were when you first had sex?

Daunting stuff, I know. But before you launch into a discussion of what goes where and why they shouldn't have sex until they're in their mid-thirties, there's some work you need to do to make the conversations more effective and go more smoothly. You need to clarify your values about sexuality, love, and relationships.

This may sound a little strange because as a child you might have had only one talk with your own nervous parent, who filled you in on the details of reproduction, told you it was for marriage, and said "Feel free to ask me if you have any questions!" and that was the first, last, and only conversation. Or perhaps you learned the "facts" without the values from your friends, a book, or at school. And then, of course, there are those of you who were self-taught and knew intuitively to never ever ask about bodies, love, relationships or, heaven forbid, sexuality or reproduction. Perhaps you looked "sex" up in the dictionary and did the best you could from there.

For most people, your own experience as a child won't do a whole lot to help you when it comes to talking about sex with your own kids. Now with sex everywhere you turn, middle school kids engaging in oral sex, and with HIV and AIDS to worry about, you may have a sense of urgency and fear fueling the desire to have open communication with your kids about sex. But you think you don't have the skills to do it "right" or you don't know where or when to start the conversations or even what to say. These concerns are enough to make a person skip the whole conversation and trust your kids' peers and the media to take care of it for you.

For many of you, the thought of explaining the mechanics of sex is a big enough deal that it's challenging to move on from there. But, sex is really so much more than just baby making, right? Talking to your kids about sex opens the door to a whole world that, in its entirety, isn't appropriate for your kids to gain full access to until they're in their teens. This isn't to say kids shouldn't have information, and lots of it, but that putting that info to use should wait.

Starting early and taking the time to have multiple brief conversations is best for everyone. You can figure out what you want your kids to know before they need to know it, and your kids will come to expect this support and information from you. If all goes well, with your guidance, your kids will make great decisions.

This guide is a resource to help you to start clarifying your values so you can effectively influence your children and their sexual decision-making from the very first conversation. According to a 2007 survey of kids age 12 to 17 by the National Campaign to Prevent Teen and Unplanned Pregnancy, parents have the most influence on kids when it comes to making decisions about dating, relationships, and sex.

Parents have the most influence on kids when it comes to making decisions about dating, relationships and sex.

Most parents think peers have the most influence, probably because of their own experiences growing up. If you think back, maybe it would have been better for you to have been able to talk openly with your parents about these things. Or maybe you were lucky and did. One thing is for sure—our kids are listening to us. They want and need our guidance when it comes to this important part of life.

Clarifying your sexual values is one important step on the way to guiding your kids through the tricky world of sexuality, love, and relationships. What do I mean by "sexual values?" Values can be defined as standards or principles in which you have some sort of emotional investment. Sexual values are what you believe about everything related to sexuality to be true for yourself and your family. Your sexual values can be influenced by your religion, your politics, your culture, your experiences, the messages you received from your parents, and your own intuitive sense of what feels right to you.

Talking about the facts and science of sexual reproduction, birth control, sexually transmitted infections (STIs), and HIV with your kids can seem overwhelming, but, lucky for you, there are many great books and websites that can help you provide this information to your kids. You don't need to be an expert on sexual health to guide your kids through discussions about the different aspects of reproduction or HIV transmission. All you really need is a basic understanding and willingness to both initiate conversations and find answers to your kids' questions. And remember, compared to your kids, you are a sex expert!

Talking about your values can be hard because there is no book you can read or website you can visit to tell you what you believe about sexuality, love, and relationships. It's up to you to clarify your values and pass them on to your kids. Some parents have a strong religious background providing clear statements about sex and sexuality. However, if your religion and personal beliefs conflict, it can make it difficult to sort out what you believe.

The idea of waiting until marriage is a perfect example. Teens need compelling reasons to wait to have sex. Just telling them to wait until they are married is probably not reason enough to convince a wildly hormonal teenager to postpone sex. If you don't believe in waiting until marriage for sex, you still need to give compelling reasons for waiting as long as possible to become sexually active. When you can explain to your child your reasoning behind your beliefs, your child may listen more closely and take time to make smarter decisions. I believe the more thoughtful your responses are to your kids, the more impact they will have.

When you know what you believe and you've clarified your own values, talking to your children about these things becomes a snap. Well, maybe not a snap, but it'll be easier. You won't fumble around trying to figure out what you believe at the same time your child is looking to you for guidance. Also, the approach you take when you talk to your kids is just as important as what you say. One of the easiest ways to figure out what to say and how to say it is to think about your own experiences as a child or teen and ask "What would have worked better for me?" This can be a great approach to help you talk with your own kids.

If you have young kids, you may find some of the topics and exercises seem too advanced for the age of your children. This guide is to help you plan for the future. If you take the time now to sort out your beliefs, as your children age, you will find you are well prepared for these conversations because you've already done at least some of the work.

Also, the sooner you clarify your sexual values and start talking to your kids, the easier it becomes. Starting these conversations when kids are young and continuing them throughout childhood and adolescence helps kids to make better decisions about sexuality, love, and relationships as they grow up. While I can't guarantee that you won't get eye rolling and sighing from your kids at some point, I can guarantee that you will feel more confident and comfortable talking about this subject!

How do you define values?

What are some of your core values that are not related to sexuality?

If your values, in general, are different from your children's other parent how can you manage these differences?

Chapter 2

LEARNING ABOUT
THE BIRDS + THE BEES

LEARNING ABOUT THE BIRDS + THE BEES

Most people have a memory of learning about sex. However you learned, the experience left some kind of impact—maybe a sense of shame or embarrassment or maybe a sense of wonder and delight. Whatever the impact, it's most likely still with you today and influences how you interact with your kids when it comes to this topic.

One parent told me she asked her mother what "rape" means. Her mother dodged the question, so she looked it up in the dictionary. This led her to the word "sex" and, what do you know, she learned the facts of life—from the dictionary! She also learned her mother wasn't a trustworthy resource and didn't bother to ask her any more questions.

Take a few moments and respond to the following questions to help you think about your experience learning about sexuality, love, and relationships when you were a kid. Describe everything you can remember in detail. What are your early memories of learning about sex? Did you learn from your parents, from your siblings or on the playground?

🐝 What were your reactions when you were a kid learning about sex? Reflect on your feelings and your thoughts at the time.

_____

_____

_____

_____

_____

_____

🐝 If you grew up in a religious family, what did your religion tell you about sex? If you were not religious, what messages did you get about sex?

_____

_____

_____

_____

_____

Describe your parents' relationship(s). Looking back, how healthy do you think they were?

What did you learn from your parents' relationship(s) that you want to pass on to your children?

What did you learn that you'd rather not pass on?

What was the message in your family about same sex relationships? If you have a gay or lesbian parent, how did you feel about this as a child? How did you feel about your family?

_____

_____

_____

_____

_____

_____

_____

If you learned about sex in school, what do you remember? How was this information helpful?

_____

_____

_____

_____

_____

_____

_____

If you were a victim of sexual abuse, how have you come to terms with this? How has this affected your relationship with your child?

_____

_____

_____

_____

_____

_____

The intention of this chapter is to help you understand how your own experiences impact and influence how you parent around sexuality. If you were sexually abused as a child, seeking counseling may help you talk to your child in a less constricted or fearful way. My hope is you will be more aware of when your personal experiences are showing up and affecting your interactions with your kids.

Chapter 3

LOVE + HEALTHY RELATIONSHIPS

LOVE + HEALTHY RELATIONSHIPS

If you've been in love at some point in your life, you may recall that it's an exciting, overwhelming, and amazing time! It's important for parents to help kids navigate these crazy wonderful feelings and make good decisions about their partners. The best way you can help your kids make good relationship choices is to be clear about what you believe the elements of a healthy relationship are and, more importantly, to model this in your own relationships —romantic and otherwise.

One important thing to remember is that your kids may be experiencing some pretty strong feelings of sexual desire. Sometimes this can be overwhelming, all-consuming and confusing. Make sure your kids understand this physical feeling is natural and healthy and help them find ways to manage it.

As you know from your own life experience, being "in love" as a teen can be very different from of being "in love" as an adult. It's important to be respectful of your teen's relationships and experiences. Allow them to experience love, whatever it looks like, without your judgment and voice of reason. For them, their experience of love is every bit as real and earth-shattering as your grown-up love. Your job is to help your teens to be as healthy and safe in the relationship as possible—not to bring them back to reality. As you well know, the course of the relationship will eventually provide them with plenty of "reality."

Think about healthy, romantic relationships and using the scale below, rate the importance of the following elements. Five equals "very important." Feel free to add any additional elements you think should be included.

Love	1	2	3	4	5
Respect	1	2	3	4	5
Trust	1	2	3	4	5
Commitment	1	2	3	4	5
Maturity	1	2	3	4	5
Communication	1	2	3	4	5
Acceptance	1	2	3	4	5

In general, what does a healthy romantic relationship look like to you?

How are you modeling healthy relationships for your children?

How could you do better?

Describe an unhealthy romantic relationship.

_____

_____

_____

_____

_____

_____

_____

_____

_____

What is the difference between lust and love?

_____

_____

_____

_____

_____

_____

The "SCRIPT!" sections are where you'll find your own way of talking about various issues with your kids.

SCRIPT! DESCRIBE AND EXPLAIN SEXUAL DESIRE.

If you are divorced or separated from your child's other parent, how does this affect your child's perception of relationships?

_____

_____

_____

_____

_____

_____

_____

_____

_____

_____

If you are a single parent, how do you manage your dating relationships?
What rules do you have for yourself about dating in relationship to your family?

_____

_____

_____

_____

_____

_____

_____

experience of sex and relationships and a woman's?

_____

_____

_____

_____

_____

What are or will be the rules about dating in your family?

_____

_____

_____

_____

_____

_____

_____

Who is responsible for setting sexual limits in a relationship and why?

_____

_____

_____

_____

_____

_____

SCRIPT! WRITE WHAT YOU WILL TELL YOUR CHILD ABOUT YOUR HOPES FOR THEIR FUTURE HEALTHY RELATIONSHIPS.

Love and relationships are very likely the most confusing parts of being a teenager. When you are able to talk clearly about your own values and beliefs about relationships, your kids will do better. They really do pay attention to us when we talk about our experiences and even offer occasional advice.

Chapter 4

WHO'S READY FOR SEX?

WHO'S READY FOR SEX?

When it comes to sexual decision making, there are so many different things that can influence the decision to have sex. Read through the list below and think about your own early sexual relationships. Add any influencing factors you believe are missing. How did these play into your sexual decision making? What did you neglect to consider when you first became sexually active? Some people didn't have a choice about the first time they had sex because they were raped or sexually abused. If this is the case for you, think about the first time you chose to have sex.

Physical maturity
Emotional maturity
Pressure (self, friends, or partner)
Fun
Consequences
Deliberate decision-making
Choice
Preparedness
Agreement and mutuality
Curiosity
Pleasure
Guilt
Alcohol and drugs
Temptation
Responsibility
Spirituality

Our kids need to have a good understanding of each of the above terms. They need to know the definition of each word and have an example they can understand. You can start teaching your kids about each of these concepts from an early age, so they have a solid understanding before they're involved in their first relationship. Once they're in their early teens, you can then talk to them about how each one of these ideas relates to sexuality and relationships.

In order to make this easier for you, complete the following exercises for each of the terms listed above.

1. *Define each term so a 6- 8 year old would understand it.*

2. *Provide a kid-friendly example that a 6-8 year old would understand.*

3. *State how it relates to sex and relationships. You will introduce this concept when your child is around age eleven.*

Example—Temptation

Definition:	Wanting to do something that may be wrong or you might feel bad about later. You can be tempted to do things you'll feel good about later too.
Example:	There are cookies on the kitchen counter. You want to eat one before dinner, but your mom said you can't have one until after dinner.
Sex and Relationships:	When you're dating someone and are kissing and fooling around, you may be tempted to have sex. It's important to know that the farther you go, the more you'll be tempted to have sex, maybe before you're ready. What could you do in a situation to help resist the temptation to have sex?

Emotional maturity

Definition:

Example:

Sex and Relationships:

Pressure (self, friends, partner)

Definition:

Example:

Sex and Relationships:

Consequences

Definition:

Example:

Sex and Relationships:

Deliberate decision-making

Definition:

Example:

Sex and Relationships:

Choice

Definition:

Example:

Sex and Relationships:

Preparedness

Definition:

Example:

Sex and Relationships:

Curiosity

Definition:

Example:

Sex and Relationships:

Pleasure

Definition:

Example:

Sex and Relationships:

Guilt

Definition:

Example:

Sex and Relationships:

Alcohol and drugs

Definition:

Example:

Sex and Relationships:

Temptation

Definition:

Example:

Sex and Relationships:

Responsibility

Definition:

Example:

Sex and Relationships:

Other:

Definition:

Example:

Sex and Relationships:

Other:
Definition:

Example:

Sex and Relationships:

Other:
Definition:

Example:

Sex and Relationships:

Whatever the age of your children, you will probably never be truly ready for them to have sex! However, by doing everything you can to help them make good decisions, you'll feel slightly more prepared for this big event.

Chapter 5

WHY WAIT?
ABSTINENCE OR POSTPONEMENT

WHY WAIT? ABSTINENCE OR POSTPONEMENT

A strong message of abstinence or postponement from parents plus information about birth control, sexually transmitted infections, and HIV and AIDS really does help kids delay sex and does increase their use of condoms and birth control. I call this "Abstinence Plus."

Providing information is not the same as giving permission.

Before you develop your own definition of abstinence, you need to define "sex." There is a continuum of intimacy from hand holding to kissing to vaginal sex to sexual activities involving multiple partners and who knows what else. Some of these activities are appropriate in public and some in private. The more specific you are in your definitions, the less room there will be for confusion.

 What is your definition of "sex?" Is it just intercourse?

_____

_____

_____

_____

_____

_____

SCRIPT! WHAT ARE YOUR CORE BELIEFS ABOUT HOW SEX INFLUENCES RELATIONSHIPS?

I know that most parents want their children to wait to have sex until they are "ready," though most of us are never truly ready for our kids to have sex. From my informal polls of parents, it seems that post high-school is the age that parents are comfortable imagining their kids jumping into the world of sexuality, love, and serious relationships.

Some parents want their children to wait until they're married. While this is a clear event and usually has firm values supporting it, it's important to include compelling reasons that support the "wait until marriage" goal. Children who are raised in religious households more often wait to have sex—but not until they are married. Unfortunately, when they do have sex for the first time, they tend to not use birth control and condoms.

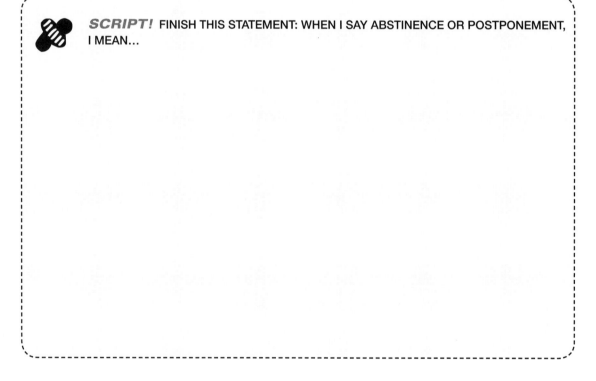

SCRIPT! FINISH THIS STATEMENT: WHEN I SAY ABSTINENCE OR POSTPONEMENT, I MEAN...

What if you had sex before marriage but now believe that sex is something reserved only for marriage? How do you talk to you kids without feeling like a hypocrite? This is really important: You don't have to reveal your sexual history to your child. You can if you want to, but it isn't required. Just as they have a right to privacy, you do, too! It is completely appropriate to stick to broad generalizations about the lessons you have learned along the way when talking about your past with your kids.

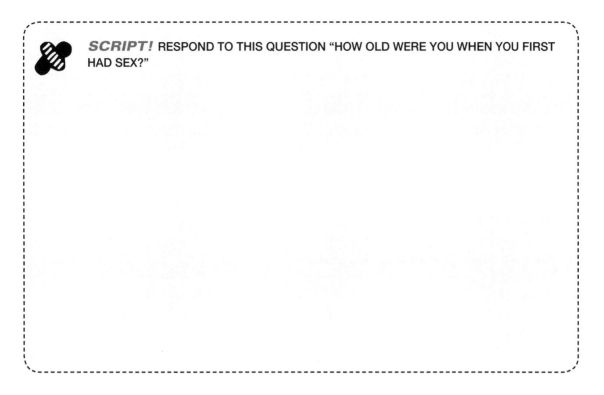

SCRIPT! RESPOND TO THIS QUESTION "HOW OLD WERE YOU WHEN YOU FIRST HAD SEX?"

For those of you who don't believe that sex is solely part of a married relationship, explaining reasons to wait to your children can seem challenging. Isn't it easier to just say "Wait until you're married" and leave it at that? Unfortunately, when you say this but don't fully believe it, your kids will eventually figure out that you weren't honest with them. Honesty is an essential part of conversations about this subject.

One way to figure out what "ready for sex" means to you is to consider your own first sexual experiences.

What was good about your first sexual experiences?

_____

_____

_____

_____

_____

_____

✿ What was bad?

_____

_____

_____

_____

_____

_____

✿ Would you repeat the experience? Why or why not?

_____

_____

_____

_____

_____

> ✿ **SCRIPT!** I THINK PEOPLE SHOULD WAIT TO HAVE SEX UNTIL... (IF YOU SAY MARRIAGE—GIVE SOME GOOD, CONCRETE REASONS TO WAIT!)

Kids need all the help they can get when it comes to making the decision to wait to have sex. They want and need to hear compelling reasons from you to wait as long as possible and they need to know how to protect themselves so they are prepared when they do have sex.

Chapter 6

TEENS + SEX

TEENS + SEX

Teens have sex, and most of us did when we were teens, too, whether we were ready for it or not. As adults and parents we have thoughts and judgments about sexually active teens that have probably changed since we were teens ourselves. Remember, if you have young kids, you will be getting a jump on the game by exploring these questions.

Spend some time thinking about your beliefs about teenagers and sex and go deeper than one-word answers.

Slightly more than one-half of adolescents have engaged in heterosexual oral sex. In fact, higher proportions of teens have engaged in this activity than have engaged in vaginal sex.

How do you feel about your teen having sex? What kind of "double standards" do you hold about boys having sex vs. girls?

How do you feel about teens using birth control without their parents' knowledge?

What do you think about girls who offer oral sex to boys they barely know?

What do you think about boys who accept offers of oral sex from girls they barely know?

How do you feel about teenagers who are sexually active but don't use birth control?

How would you feel if your teen contracted a sexually transmitted infection? What if it was incurable or required lifetime concern and care, like herpes?

What do you think about parents who allow their kids to have sex in their home? Would you?

Circle "should" or "should not":

Teenagers **should/should not** be allowed to have sex in their own home.

Teenagers **should/should not** be able to get birth control without parental consent.

Teenagers **should/should not** be able to get STI and HIV testing without parental consent.

Teenagers **should/should not** be able to terminate a pregnancy without parental consent.

Teenagers **should/should not** date people three or more years older than they are.

Teenagers **should/should not** become parents.

When you know what you believe about teen sexuality, have thought about it, and talked with your friends and family about it, you'll feel better about your own teen's sexuality. If your kids are young and you are wondering how this is helpful to you now, remember—you have a jump on the game. You won't have to do this work in the heat of the moment because you know what your values are now.

Chapter 7

SEXUALLY TRANSMITTED INFECTIONS + HIV

SEXUALLY TRANSMITTED INFECTIONS + HIV

In this day and age of HIV and AIDS, we must talk to our kids about sexually transmitted infections—and sooner than we think! If you watch the news or listen to the radio when your kids are around, they have most likely heard the words and possibly engaged in discussion with friends about AIDS. If your child has started puberty, he or she should know that people can sometimes pass germs and can become very sick from having sex. Perhaps this will act as a deterrent to sexual activity! Every little nudge towards waiting to have sex is a good one, right?

At the end of 2006 young people ages 13-24 comprised about 16 percent of all HIV infections. This was up from 13% in 2003.

You don't need to know every little detail of each infection, but it's helpful to have a basic understanding of symptoms, methods of transmission and whether they are treatable. The American Social Health Association website is a good place to start if you need more information. See the resources section for more information.

Remember! The best way to prevent an STI or HIV is to abstain from sex of any kind—oral, anal, and vaginal. The second best way is to use a condom every time you have sex. Finally, long-term monogamy with an honest and faithful partner is also very effective.

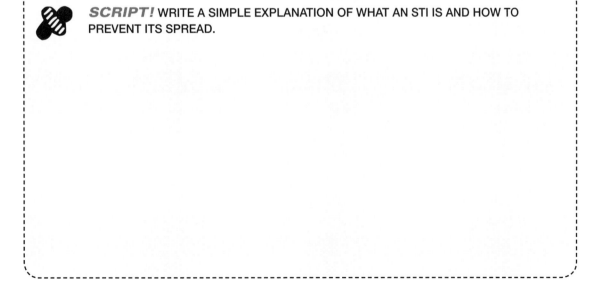

SCRIPT! WRITE A SIMPLE EXPLANATION OF WHAT AN STI IS AND HOW TO PREVENT ITS SPREAD.

I'm going to make it a little easier and provide a simple, starter script for discussing HIV and AIDS. This is vitally important information for your children to have, and it's important that the information you give them is accurate. It's best to have this conversation by about age 10.

> "There is a Sexually Transmitted Infection called HIV that causes an illness called AIDS. It's caused by a virus or germ that travels from person to person in body fluids—blood, semen, vaginal secretions, and breast milk.
>
> The HIV virus eats away at the immune system that usually keeps us healthy. The white blood cells can't fight off regular illnesses and diseases, and a person with HIV eventually develops AIDS.
>
> It's sad because AIDS causes the person to die. There is no cure right now, but people can take medicines that help them to be healthy and live as long as possible.
>
> Having sexual intercourse with an infected partner is one way to get HIV. This means vaginal, anal, or oral sex. You can also get HIV from sharing needles to inject drugs.
>
> The best way to prevent HIV infection is to not have sex and not use intravenous drugs. If you decide to have sex, using a condom every time can stop you from becoming infected with HIV. Also, having only one partner who does not have sex with other people can prevent HIV."

This is just to get you started. The Sexuality Information and Education Council of the United States provides excellent information about how to talk to kids of all ages about HIV and AIDS. See the resources section for more information.

 SCRIPT! EXPLAIN WHAT A CONDOM IS AND HOW TO USE IT.

Safer sex means sexual activity that does not involve any exchange of body fluids—semen, vaginal secretions, blood, or breast milk. Kissing, touching, sexual talk, sex with a condom, and sex within a mutually monogamous relationship are examples of safer sex activities.

SCRIPT! WHAT WILL YOU SAY TO REASSURE YOUR KIDS ABOUT DECIDING TO HAVE SEX AND THE POSSIBILITY OF CONTRACTING AN STI OR BECOMING PREGNANT?

Do you know anyone who has HIV or AIDS? What do you think about them and their circumstances?

- **There is vaccine available for the Human Papillomavirus (HPV), an STI that causes cervical cancer. In order for it to be effective, it needs to be given before people become sexually active, by about age 11. What do you think about this vaccine? Would you give it to your child? Why or why not?**

- **What will you say to your child if they confide in you that they have contracted an STI?**

Sexually Transmitted Infections, HIV, and AIDS can be really scary to think about—especially when you think about the risks you know teenagers take. Thinking about talking to your younger child about STIs and HIV is also a frightening prospect. Remember, when you provide this information in a loving, supportive, non-threatening way, your kids will be considerably less frightened than if they learn through misinformation from their peers.

Chapter 8
BIRTH CONTROL

BIRTH CONTROL

The only form of birth control that is 100% effective is abstinence. While there are many other forms of birth control, this is the only method guaranteed to work effectively every time it's used. Unfortunately, practicing abstinence is really hard to do when your hormones are raging. Most of us have been there, and even as adults we've probably made choices that weren't the smartest when it came to pregnancy and STI protection.

The problem with abstinence is when it fails, it fails miserably. Even if you strongly believe sex is reserved only for marriage and have made this very clear to your kids, most research shows that kids want and need to know about birth control. The fact is, what works best for kids is a strong message of abstinence plus information about birth control and STIs.

What works best for kids is a strong message of abstinence plus information about birth control and STIs.

Providing information about birth control is not the same as giving permission to use it. It's just smart, because I don't think there is a parent out there who would wish an unplanned pregnancy on their teenaged kid. I am hopeful that you would rather be really angry and disappointed in your children's choices rather than deal with an unplanned pregnancy.

I'm not going to discuss every method of birth control—you can easily find that information from a variety of sources. I want you to explore your beliefs about birth control and how you will talk to your kids about it.

Finally, in this time of HIV and AIDS kids need to know that when they have sex, they should use a condom every time—even if they are using another form of birth control. Other than abstinence, condoms are the best way to prevent the transmission of STIs and HIV. When you say "sex," say "condom," every time. The two should go together like bread and butter.

SCRIPT! EXPLAIN WHAT BIRTH CONTROL IS FOR AND WHY PEOPLE USE IT.

Respond to the following statements and questions.

My religion says using birth control is **good/bad/neutral/don't know**
and I **agree/disagree** with this because…

_____

_____

_____

_____

I want my daughter to be protected from pregnancy.   **True/False**

I believe birth control is morally wrong. **True/False**

I will help my daughter get birth control before she needs it. **True/False**

I will make sure my kids know about and understand how to use every form of
birth control that's currently available. **True/False**

I will have condoms available in my home for my children to use, no questions
asked. **True/False**

I will take my children to get birth control if they ask me to. **True/False**

I will make sure my children know where to get birth control if they need it.
True/False

🎗 Is there anything else you want your kids to know about birth control?

_____

_____

_____

_____

_____

_____

_____

_____

_____

🎗 What will you do if you find out your child is sexually active and NOT using birth control?

_____

_____

_____

_____

_____

_____

_____

_____

_____

🎗 What will you do if you suspect your child is sexually active, but you don't believe in using birth control?

_____

_____

_____

_____

_____

_____

_____

✍ How do you think alcohol consumption influences the use of birth control and condoms?

_____

_____

_____

_____

_____

_____

_____

_____

When kids have information about birth control, their risk of unplanned pregnancy goes down. Just because children have information about birth control it doesn't mean they think they now have permission to have sex. It just means they are more likely to use it when they become sexually active.

Chapter 9

PREGNANCY, ADOPTION, ABORTION + AND ALL THAT

PREGNANCY, ABORTION, ADOPTION + ALL THAT

Conception or fertilization is the moment the egg and sperm connect in the fallopian tube, and pregnancy begins when the fertilized egg implants in the uterine wall.

Unplanned pregnancy is a fact of life, and I think it's safe to say that no parents want their children to experience pregnancy before they're ready. Talking about your beliefs about teen pregnancy, conception, abortion and adoption are some of the most important conversations you can have with your kids.

SCRIPT! EXPLAIN WHY PEOPLE GIVE CHILDREN UP FOR ADOPTION.

Do you believe life begins at conception? Why or why not?

_____

_____

_____

_____

What do you believe about abortion?

Why do women make the choice to have an abortion?

What do you think about women who have abortions?

- Do you believe abortion is acceptable only in some circumstances, such as incest or rape? Why or why not?

- How would you feel if your child chose to have an abortion?

- If you know someone who has had an abortion, what do you think about them and their decision?

At least half of American women will experience an unintended pregnancy by age 45, and, at current rates, about one-third will have had an abortion.

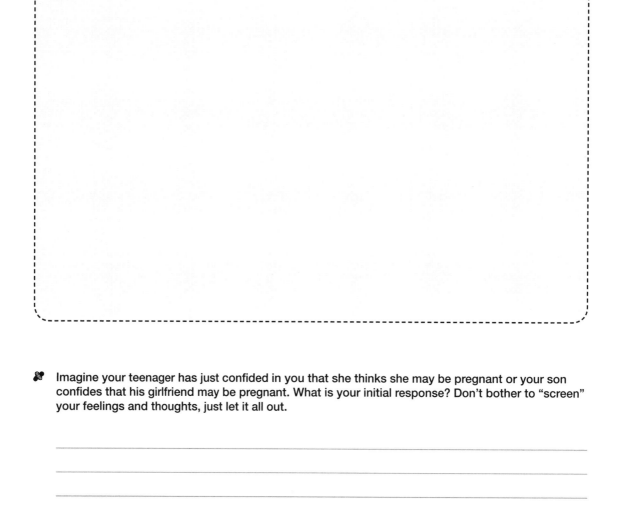

SCRIPT! EXPLAIN ABORTION TO YOUR KIDS—WHAT IT IS AND YOUR VALUES ABOUT IT.

Imagine your teenager has just confided in you that she thinks she may be pregnant or your son confides that his girlfriend may be pregnant. What is your initial response? Don't bother to "screen" your feelings and thoughts, just let it all out.

It's probably safe to assume that at least some of what you wrote above isn't going to be particularly helpful to your teenager. What would be helpful to your teen? What would you want to hear if you were in his or her shoes or what did you want to hear if you were in that same situation when you were a teen?

_____

_____

_____

_____

_____

_____

_____

_____

_____

If your teen, or his girlfriend, has decided to end the pregnancy, what could you say?

_____

_____

_____

_____

_____

_____

_____

_____

_____

If your teen, or his girlfriend, has decided adoption is the solution to this pregnancy, what could you say?

_____

_____

_____

_____

_____

What could you say if your teen, or his girlfriend, has decided to keep the baby?

_____

_____

_____

_____

_____

_____

_____

SCRIPT! WHAT WILL YOU SAY TO YOUR CHILDREN ABOUT BEING TEEN PARENTS?

This exercise is intended to get you thinking about teen pregnancy and your beliefs about it, so you can find ways to talk about it in a thoughtful way. If your child does become pregnant or impregnates someone, your reaction may surprise you, but if you have already been talking about your beliefs and values, your reaction may not be a surprise to your teen. This may help pave the way for an easier conversation about the situation, should it arise. And hopefully it won't!

Chapter 10

SELF STIMULATION
+ MASTURBATION

SELF STIMULATION + MASTURBATION

What an amazing thing, the human body! Our kids think they are pretty amazing too, and once they figure out that it feels good when they touch their penis or clitoris—watch out! Kids under 5 will self-stimulate whenever and wherever. If it feels good, why not do it?

Babies and young children "self-stimulate"—it just feels good to touch their privates, and they do it for stress relief and to self-soothe. Masturbation involves fantasy and ideally, privacy. It's important for kids to know that it's normal to masturbate and also normal not to. Children can start to masturbate by about 8 or 9. If self stimulation or masturbation involves others, is interrupting regular play, or becomes a central activity, it might be time to talk to a professional. This isn't typical behavior in kids.

How we react when young kids self-stimulate is very important. Because we want them to know we are trustworthy and safe to talk to about bodies, sexuality and, well, anything, it's really important to remain calm, cool, and collected when this is going on. This means no yelling, shaming, or blaming, even if you believe self-stimulation and masturbation are always inappropriate.

If we yell at kids when they are engaged in any kind of "sexual behavior," especially young children, they learn that we can't handle this kind of behavior, so it may go underground. They will make an effort to keep us from being upset. This could mean your child won't tell you if something really scary is happening, for example, that someone is sexually abusing them.

We can teach them in a loving way that this is something people do in private and alone. It's important to say "alone" because little kids think being at home on the couch watching TV is private.

🌀 What was the message you received in childhood about self-stimulation and masturbation?

_____

_____

_____

_____

_____

_____

What are your beliefs about it now?

SCRIPT! WRITE A STATEMENT ABOUT SELF STIMULATION AND MASTURBATION THAT INCLUDES A MESSAGE ABOUT PRIVACY AND YOUR BELIEFS.

Most of us are pretty uncomfortable when it comes to talking about masturbation. It's one of those things that pretty much everybody does and no one talks about. Openness about this topic can help your kids to feel "normal"—something every kid worries about at one time or another.

Chapter 11

"PLAYING DOCTOR" + BEYOND—CHILDHOOD SEXUAL BEHAVIOR

"PLAYING DOCTOR" + BEYOND—CHILDHOOD SEXUAL BEHAVIOR

General Childhood Sexual Development

Kids are naturally curious about their own bodies and each other's. After all, what could be more interesting than a penis if you don't have one or have never seen one? A certain amount of "playing doctor" or body exploration is perfectly normal and natural throughout childhood.

Parents of preschoolers get to hear a lot of potty talk, questions about pregnancy and birth, and conversations and comments relating to differences in body parts. Showing and looking at private body parts and self-stimulation in public and private are also part of the fun. Occasionally kids will touch each other's privates, usually out of curiosity, not because they are trying to sexually stimulate in some way.

All of the above is developmentally normal, and just because it's natural and healthy, doesn't mean we have to be comfortable with it. However, as parents who want their children to be comfortable talking to us about any and everything, we need to be careful about monitoring our sometimes-strong reactions to their normal sexual play.

Sometimes this behavior can cross the line and become "sexualized" which means, essentially, it's adult-like. Usually the child is imitating something they have seen or that they have physically experienced themselves. This behavior is not natural and healthy, and I would recommend close monitoring and consultation with a professional as it can indicate sexual abuse. Not always, however, so don't immediately assume the worst.

Natural and healthy sexual play is spontaneous, mutual, and good humored. It spontaneously emerges out of play and looks like play; both kids agree to play this way without threats or coercion; and they are having fun. This is a quick and easy way for your to determine if you need to worry about the behavior.

When to worry: Imitating adults sexually (sexualized play); sex play using force, threats, dominance, violence, aggression; and/or compulsiveness. Remember, children who are engaging in sexualized play may need help, and their parents should be contacted.

One of the most important ways for you to determine just how concerned you should be is your intuition. If you have that "uh-oh" or gut feeling that something is wrong, 9 times out of 10, you will be right. Trust your gut—it is your ally.

Children continue to explore each other's bodies throughout their childhood and adolescence. As elementary-aged kids, this usually takes the form of role playing games and some mild experimentation.

As kids enter puberty, usually around 11 or so, their exploration becomes more adult-like, including kissing, body rubbing, and very occasionally actual intercourse. Once kids are fully into adolescence, 13 to 16, everything goes.

Kids need information about okay touch and not-okay touch, and regular reminders about keeping their bodies safe. They need to know that they are the "boss" of their body and have the right to say no to any kind of play, sexual or otherwise. Young kids also need to know about reproductive biology because it gives them a reference point for sexual activity, i.e., it's something adults do, not kids.

If we yell at kids when they are engaged in any kind of "sexual behavior," especially young children, they learn that we can't handle this kind of behavior, so it may go underground. They will make an effort to keep us from being upset. This could mean your child won't tell you if something really scary is happening.

When kids know about sexual intercourse, they are safer. Sexual predators look for kids who are "innocent" and don't have open relationships with their parents.

It's pretty much safe to say most parents are terrified their child will be sexually abused. Part of this fear comes from our own experiences and part from the number of stories we hear in the news, on TV, and the internet about "stranger danger," sexual abuse, exploitation, and abduction. It seems like a potential abuser is lurking on every corner.

Sadly, the majority of sexual abusers are known to the child, and the idea of "stranger danger" is bunk. Make sure your kids know they can tell you if something bad happens to them. They need to hear that you are available to them. And more than that, they need to see it.

This means not freaking out when they are "playing doctor" or touching their privates. When you remain calm in these moments, our kids learn we can handle this kind of body stuff. When we freak out, they learn that we can't handle it, and the behavior can go underground.

Besides not freaking out, the best thing you can do for your kids is to teach them from an early age they are the boss of their bodies. They have the right to say no (and loudly) if someone touches them in a way they don't like or feels uncomfortable. Of course there are times when you or a doctor or nurse will need to touch their penis or vulva, but make sure they understand this is for a reason—they are hurting or sick or just to make sure everything is fine.

When our kids have clear boundaries, know what words to use, and have loving, open parents, they are safer. When they know about sexuality, how babies are made, the names of their private body parts (penis, scrotum, vulva and vagina), and that sex is for not for kids, they are safer. And when they are older and can talk to you about the tricky world of sexuality and sexual feelings, they are safer.

Here is a simple script you can use with your kids when they are engaging in any type of sexual play—even if you catch your teenager in the living room having sex! Please be sure to make these words your own. This script is just a guideline to give a basic understanding of the language that generally works best when interacting with kids.

Your tone should be calm—even if you are completely freaked out—because you want your kids to know you can handle anything that comes your way. No yelling, shaming, blaming, or being big and scary (if you can help it!).

You may need to repeat the steps a few times with the kids before they get fully redirected from this behavior. If the behavior is adult-like in any way, or if it just isn't stopping, I'd recommend you contact one of the resources at the end of the book for more help.

Step 1: Describe the behavior - "I see you and Billy are looking at each other's penises."

Step 2: Describe your reaction - "I feel uncomfortable when this happens."

Step 3: Redirect - "Why don't you pull up your pants and let's go play outside. We'll talk about this later."

Step 4: Regroup—Ask yourself , "What just happened here? What is my intuition telling me? "

Step 5: Plan—Ask yourself, "What do I need to do next?" This step always includes telling the other parent the kids were "playing doctor". Depending on the behavior, it may include a call to child protective services. Remember to have a conversation about okay touch with your child after you have calmed down.

If the behavior continues, start with "I've told you this before..." and between Step 1 and 2 add "This needs to stop and we'll talk about this later." Be clear, kind and firm, but not mean or threatening.

This script really will work for kids of any age—just substitute "making out on the couch" for "looking at each other's penises" and you are good to go. Remember to stay calm, cool, and collected and you'll be able to manage yourself and the situation with grace.

Adolescent Sexual Behaviors

Teenagers these days are engaging in a lot of sexual behavior that can be adult-like and quite startling to parents. For example, imitating sex on the dance floor, called "freak dancing" or "sex dancing" is happening at nearly every Middle and High School dance. This is when the boy stands behind the girl who, while dancing, provocatively bends over as the boy is dancing and sometimes rubbing against her. It looks like sex—a lot like sex.

✷ What would you like your kids to know about this type of dancing?

_____

_____

_____

_____

_____

_____

_____

Teens are also sending sexually provocative text messages and photographs—"sexting." When anyone, including the child herself, sends sexually graphic pictures of a minor, it's considered trafficking child pornography.

✷ How would you explain the risks of texting these types of messages and photos. Consider both the social, emotional and legal consequences.

_____

_____

_____

_____

_____

_____

_____

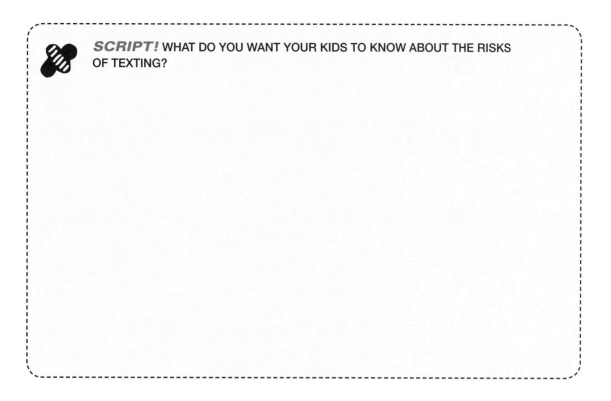

SCRIPT! WHAT DO YOU WANT YOUR KIDS TO KNOW ABOUT THE RISKS OF TEXTING?

Overtly sexual pictures or statements on social networking sites can also be a problem for teens. This can put them at risk for predatory behavior, bullying, teasing, and sexual harassment.

How comfortable are you keeping tabs on your child's social networking sites like MySpace and FaceBook? Is this something you do (or will do?)? Why or why not?

Don't feel bad if the information in this chapter is new to you or if you've yelled at your kids when they have been exploring. Most of our personal experience around natural behavior wasn't positive, so we aren't well prepared to handle this behavior by our own kids. If you were sexually abused, these behaviors can be even more challenging for you.

Chapter 12

CHANGING BODY— CHANGING MIND

CHANGING BODY—CHANGING MIND

When she started to develop breasts, a woman I know thought she had breast cancer because she felt the lump of the mammary gland and breast tissue. No one told her this was normal, and she didn't have anyone to ask!

We all have memories of when our bodies began to go through puberty and adolescence—the process of physically and psychologically changing from a child to an adult. Maybe you found this to be an exciting time or maybe it was confusing to you. Perhaps you had a book explaining the process or you watched a film at school while separated from the opposite sex.

Or maybe you had no information at all and were surprised to discover that you were bleeding "down there" for no good reason. Or perhaps you had a wet dream and had no idea what was going on. Whatever your experience—good, bad or ugly—it will probably impact your experience of your child's changing body and changing mind.

🦴 When and how did you learn about the changes of puberty? Write down some of your earliest memories of your changing body.

_____

_____

_____

_____

_____

_____

_____

🦴 Was there anything that confused or scared you?

_____

_____

_____

_____

_____

How did your parents react when you began puberty?

What do you remember about your emotional state at this time?

What did you want to hear from your parents about this time in your life?

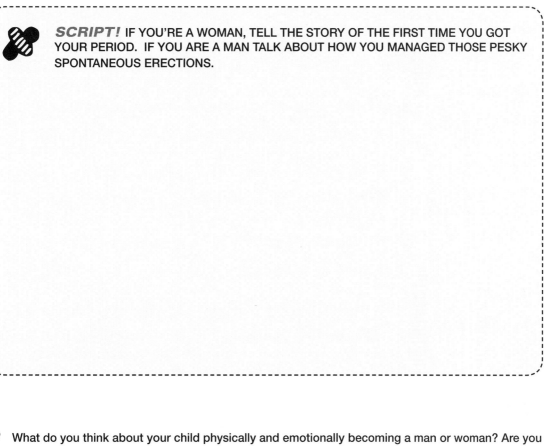

SCRIPT! IF YOU'RE A WOMAN, TELL THE STORY OF THE FIRST TIME YOU GOT YOUR PERIOD. IF YOU ARE A MAN TALK ABOUT HOW YOU MANAGED THOSE PESKY SPONTANEOUS ERECTIONS.

What do you think about your child physically and emotionally becoming a man or woman? Are you looking forward to these changes? Why or why not?

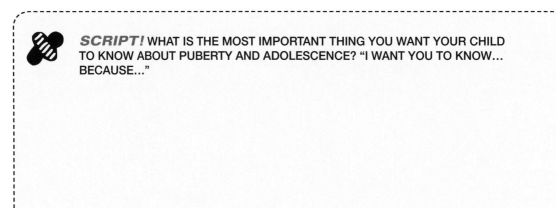

SCRIPT! WHAT IS THE MOST IMPORTANT THING YOU WANT YOUR CHILD TO KNOW ABOUT PUBERTY AND ADOLESCENCE? "I WANT YOU TO KNOW... BECAUSE..."

Puberty and adolescence is a challenging time for both parents and kids. The more you can prepare yourself for this change of life, the better, and remember—they are just as baffled by the changes in their body, mind, and attitude as you may be.

Chapter 13

SAME SEX RELATIONSHIPS + SEXUAL ORIENTATION

SAME SEX RELATIONSHIPS + SEXUAL ORIENTATION

Same sex relationships and sexual orientation are a part life, and it's important you talk to your kids about them. Whether you believe being gay is totally and completely fine or totally and completely wrong or somewhere in between, it's important for children to know about same sex relationships and sexual orientation. If you are a gay or lesbian parent, then you know how important and impactful parents' reactions to this can be. I believe kids need to know about sexual attraction and how it's possible to be attracted to someone who is the same sex, opposite sex or both. Most kids want to know they are normal and it's our job to help them with this.

Sexual orientation means whom you are sexually attracted to—someone of the same sex, opposite sex, or both.

A word of caution—because you can't tell by looking if a person is gay or lesbian (and this includes your own kids), it's important to discuss this topic with care and sensitivity, no matter what you believe. If your child is gay and you believe this is wrong, the last thing your child needs is to think you will hate him or her because of this. Most gay people will tell you that their attraction to the same sex is not a choice.

The most important thing when discussing this issue is to remain in communication with your child. Gay teens have a higher rate of suicide, and open communication and support from you can make this very personal and sometimes difficult discovery easier. As you can imagine, it is difficult to be gay in our culture, and the more supportive you can be to your kid, the better off the child will be.

As part of natural and healthy sexual behavior, sometimes kids engage in role playing games involving some sexual experimentation, usually between the ages of 6 and 12. Two girls playing a game of "wedding" need someone to be the groom. If the game progresses to the honeymoon night, some experimentation can occur. Because the girls are the same sex, this does not make either or both of them gay. It's most likely a matter of availability.

If you are a gay or lesbian parent, what are your particular parenting challenges or concerns?

_____

_____

_____

_____

_____

_____

_____

What do you remember about learning what it means to be gay or lesbian?

_____

_____

_____

_____

_____

_____

_____

_____

SCRIPT! EXPLAIN WHAT "GAY" MEANS AND YOUR BELIEFS ABOUT SAME SEX RELATIONSHIPS.

What was the message in your family about being gay or lesbian?

_____

_____

_____

_____

_____

_____

_____

SCRIPT! WHAT WILL YOU SAY TO YOUR CHILDREN IF THEY THINK THEY ARE GAY OR LESBIAN?

Considering the world we live in, even your very young child can understand why their friend has two mommies or daddies. Introducing the idea of same sex relationships and your values early helps kids make sense of the world.

Chapter 14

PORNOGRAPHY + THE INTERNET

PORNOGRAPHY + THE INTERNET

These days, we can't talk about pornography without talking about the internet. The two are forever linked, and now porn is accessible without even trying to find it. Pornographers don't care about your child or your values. They want to hook people—no matter their age—so they can make money. Gone are the days of sneaking peeks at somebody's father's Playboy magazine and worrying about getting caught.

The internet is the crack cocaine of pornography—easy to get and highly addictive.

It has become important to have explicit conversations with our kids about pornography by approximately age 9, because it is so easy to find, and it can be highly addictive. They need to know what it is and your beliefs and values about it, especially as it relates to kids. They need to know what to do when they encounter it accidentally or when friends show them porn sites.

You also need to control access to your computer. This means having the computer in a public place, using parental controls to ensure your child doesn't accidently (or purposefully) look at porn sites. You need to check your child's history on the computer and discuss internet safety regularly. It's possible to go from looking for "big boobies" to bestiality in a few keystrokes.

Viewing sexually explicit imagery before a person is psychologically ready can be confusing, stimulating and scary—possibly creating the opposite of a healthy relationship with sex and sexuality. Because the teen brain is still developing, when kids masturbate using porn, I believe this can do more harm than good. It can also become addictive and lead to lifelong problems. It can set up unrealistic expectations about sex and make real sexual encounters confusing and less appealing.

After you finish this book or this section of the book, please take some time to learn about pornography and its influence on our relationships, culture, women, men, and families. Check the resources section for some great books and websites.

Pornography is sexually explicit pictures, film, writing, or other material, and the primary purpose is to cause sexual arousal.

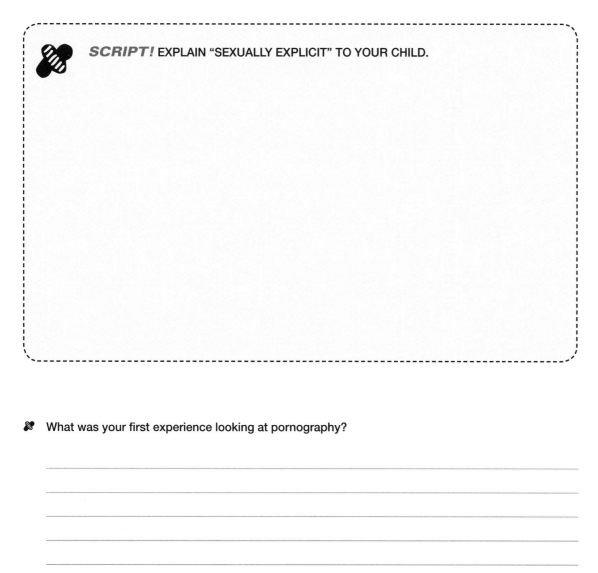

SCRIPT! EXPLAIN "SEXUALLY EXPLICIT" TO YOUR CHILD.

What was your first experience looking at pornography?

What do you remember thinking and/or feeling when you looked at porn for the first time?

- What is your current relationship with pornography?

- Do you believe viewing pornography is healthy? Why or why not?

- Why do some people find pornography appealing?

How does pornography effect:

Men -

Women -

Children and Teenagers -

Relationships -

How do you think pornography impacts people's expectations about sex and sexual relationships?

_____

_____

_____

_____

_____

SCRIPT! PROVIDE A SCRIPT FOR YOUR CHILDREN TO USE IF THEY ENCOUNTER PORNOGRAPHY AT A FRIEND'S HOUSE.

- Viewing porn can feel good to teens. What are few other ways teens can deal with their sexual feelings?

- What are your family rules about the internet? Create them now if don't already have some.

- Explain why you have these rules.

Whatever you believe about pornography, it's important to talk about it and talk about safe use of the internet on a regular basis. Kids need to be reminded of our values and beliefs —they forget!

Chapter 15

MEDIA + YOUR KIDS

MEDIA AND YOUR KIDS

While our kids are bombarded with media messages wherever they go, most of the media exposure is at home, in front of their own televisions. Kids in the U.S. watch an average of four hours of television every day. According to a study by the Kaiser Family Foundation, 70% of all television programs have some content related to sex—characters talk about it, joke about it, or engage in it.

Because most of us don't watch every moment of TV with our kids, this means they're bombarded with messages about sexuality, love, and relationships consistently but without our values attached to these messages. They're learning what it means to be a boy or a girl, how to talk to the opposite sex, values about dating, marriage, and, on very rare occasions, how to practice safer sex.

Except for sleeping, children ages 8 to 18, spend more time in front of computer, television, and game screens than any other activity. This is as much time as the average adult spends at work.

Our kids are also learning which products to buy and how to dress. For girls this is particularly challenging, because they're exposed to messages about sexuality at a very early age, and because of this, young girls can start dressing and behaving like teenagers. Perhaps you've noticed young girls dressing like teenagers in low-slung jeans, midriff-baring tops, and high heeled boots. This is an example of the sexualization of young girls; they look and dress in a manner beyond their years. It can be very confusing for girls, especially if they attract attention of a sexual nature before they are prepared to deal with it.

Our boys are not immune to this phenomenon. They are watching the girls in their classes and learning, right along with them, what it means to be valuable as a girl or woman in our culture. I can't help but wonder what they are thinking and deciding about girls when they see them dressed in provocative clothing. Boys also learn that "getting" sex is an important goal, and this idea is presented to them repeatedly in the media.

It's important we talk about these messages with our kids so we can help them navigate our increasingly confusing world. When they are able to understand that what they see on TV isn't reality, we equip them to make better choices.

What kind of media are your kids exposed to - TV shows, video games, and movies?

What do you think your kids are learning from these shows?

What are three things you could discuss with your children after viewing sexual content on TV?

What are your family rules about television viewing? Don't have any?
Make some up!

_____

_____

_____

_____

_____

_____

What are your family rules about clothing? Don't have any? Make some up!

_____

_____

_____

_____

_____

SCRIPT! WHAT DO YOU WANT YOUR KIDS TO KNOW ABOUT HOW MEDIA
INFLUENCES THEIR DECISION MAKING?

Media and its influence are nearly impossible for you to avoid.
Even if you restrict screen time, your kids will be exposed to all
sorts of things. It's not your fault. Read *So Sexy, So Soon—The
New Sexualized Childhood and What Parents Can Do to Protect
Their Kids* for more information and support about this topic. It's
in the resources section.

Chapter 16
WHAT'S NEXT?

WHAT'S NEXT?

The answer to this depends on where you are in the conversation with your kids. If you have yet to start the conversation, it's most likely time to start. If you have been talking to your kids for a while, but haven't been thoughtfully including your values in the conversations, now you can!

   Kids are ready and able to learn the basics of reproduction at about age five or six. I know, I know, this seems young! There are several reasons why I believe starting the conversation so early is beneficial.

- They're usually entering kindergarten and will be meeting and interacting with all kinds of kids who have all kinds of information. Your child needs to have the necessary information from you because you're a trustworthy source, unlike an older child on the playground.

- They're blank slates. While children have innate sexual feelings, they usually don't know what we know about sexuality, love and relationships. They don't know to be embarrassed or ashamed. They don't know what it means to be in a sexual relationship. Ideally, they don't know about rape, porn, or sexual abuse. They learn about sex like anything else they're interested in - such as volcanoes or horses—with openness and curiosity.

- Kids who know about sex are offered some protection from sexual abuse. Sexual abusers look for children who are "innocent." When children know sex is not for kids, because you've told them so, there's a higher likelihood they'll resist the behavior and be more likely to tell you if it happens.

- Starting age-appropriate conversations early makes more involved conversations about this subject much easier for you later on. Talking about the facts of reproduction, puberty, STIs, and HIV with your young kid is much easier than talking to your "madly in love" fourteen-year-old about waiting to have sex. Starting the conversations at a young age gives you many years of practice before adolescence.

Tips for Starting the Conversation

- Get a book. Read with your children if they're under the age of seven. If they're older, they may not be willing to read with you. Be sure to read the book yourself before you hand it off to your kids. Your kid will eventually read the book—there isn't a kid on the planet that doesn't have questions. See the resources page for age-appropriate book suggestions.

- Don't make a big event out of it! Throw a book in with the regular nightly reading; bring it up in the car as you are headed to the grocery store or as you are tucking them in at night.

- Take advantage of "teachable moments." Pregnant friends, teachers, celebrities, TV and movies, their friends who date, and HIV and AIDS in the news can all be catalysts for conversations with your kids.

- Don't wait for your child to ask you about sex. It's your job to initiate these conversations! When you wait for them to ask, you're making them responsible for their sexual health education. This isn't their job—it's yours (for better or worse!).

- Apologize to your older (9+) kids for not talking to them sooner. Say "I'm sorry we haven't talked about this before. I feel a little uncomfortable, and you might, too, but this is important stuff, so we'll be talking about it from now on."

- Be brave and ask your older kids what they know or remember about baby making, stages of puberty, or STIs and HIV. This is a great way to get the conversation started with older kids.

- Divide the labor. If you are comfortable talking about sex, STIs, and HIV, all the scientific stuff, and your spouse isn't, make dating and relationships his or her responsibility.

- Script answers to the topics you are most terrified of discussing. You might have covered some of them here, but make sure you have your top 5-10 ready to go.

Tips for Continuing the Conversations

- Remember, this isn't one long conversation. It is a series of short and sweet conversations throughout childhood and adolescence.

- Give "Public Service Announcements" as you are driving. Remind your kids of your values as you head to the grocery store. Be funny about it, not preachy— they will listen to you.

- Plan what you will say before you say it. Make a script and practice when you're alone in your car. Scripts aren't cheating—they're smart!

- If your kids are unwilling to talk to you, tell them you need two minutes of their time and have them time you. Then tell your kids what you want them to know. If they don't stop you from talking, don't go over five minutes because you don't want them to be overwhelmed with information.

- You don't have to know everything—just be willing to find out the answers when you don't know, and be willing to talk to your kids.

- Don't worry about providing too much information. Well meaning parents really can't do much damage to their kids. Try to keep the conversations age-appropriate and trust your instincts. No one will die if your seven-year-old knows about condoms.

- Repeat yourself. Kids don't remember every little detail, so it's your job to give them the same information several times throughout their childhood and adolescence.

- Ask open ended questions like "What do you think about the kids you know who are having sex?" or "When do you think it's an okay time to become sexually active?" or "What do you think 'sexy' means?"

- Talk about what you remember about having crushes, your first boy- or girlfriend, your friend's relationships, and dating. They like to hear our stories.

- Make sure your kids have a trustworthy adult they can confide in that isn't you or their other parent This could be your sister, brother, best friend, or anyone who shares your values. Chances are good they will come to this adult first to test the waters.

- Finally, relax! You can handle these conversations and the pay-off can be huge.

Chapter 17
IN CLOSING

IN CLOSING

I love these last two questions, and I encourage you to keep your focus on your hopes, rather than our cultural messages, your experiences as a kid, and what the neighbors might think. You will serve your kids well if you know and talk about your hopes and expectations for their future.

When you think about sexuality, love, and relationships, what are your hopes for your child?

When you think about talking to your child about sexuality, love, and relationships, what are your hopes for yourself?

When you talk to your kids about your sexual values, you teach them how to communicate, to manage themselves under pressure and, to use good decision-making skills. These gifts will last a lifetime and serve them in a variety of situations, not just where sex is concerned. If you can talk to your kids about sex, you can talk to them about anything! And if you can talk to your kids about anything, chances are good your kids will make better choices and lead happier lives.

And who wouldn't want that?

Chapter 18

RESOURCES

RECOMMENDED READING FOR KIDS

For ages 3 to 8

It's MY Body—A Book to Teach Young Children How to Resist Uncomfortable Touch
Lory Freeman
This simple book for young children provides straightforward scenarios and scripts for kids to use for how to deal with uncomfortable touch. A classic book by Parenting Press.

Your Body Belongs to You
Cornelia Spelman and Teri Weidner
This lovely book addresses what to do and say if someone touches you in a way you don't like. It's a simple, non-threatening discussion of sexual abuse for kids ages 6 to 10.

It's Not the Stork: A Book About Girls, Boys, Babies, Bodies, Families and Friends
Robie H. Harris and Michael Emberley
A wonderful book for younger children, this book provides the right amount of information to satisfy preschoolers' curiosity.

What's the Big Secret? Talking about Sex with Girls and Boys
Laurie Krasny Brown, Ed.D. and Mark Brown
This book for young children introduces the basics of body differences, baby making, pregnancy, birth, and good and bad touches. It's thoughtfully written and illustrated by the creator of Arthur and his spouse.

It's So Amazing! A Book about Eggs, Sperm, Birth, Babies and Families
Robie Harris and Michael Emberley
This is my all-time favorite book about sex, for kids 5 to 11. It has great comic-book-style illustrations and detailed information about pregnancy, birth, sex, bodies, families, keeping safe, HIV, and love. Your kids will refer back to this book over and over again.

Where Did I Come From?
Peter Mayle
The classic 1970's book for kids ages 7 and older. It has funny, chubby characters and frank discussion of sex, pregnancy, birth, and all that goes along with this topic.

For ages 8 and older

My Body Is Private
Linda Walvoord Girard
Another book about touching for older kids, this one explains sexual abuse without using those words. It gives kids ideas for what to do if someone touches them inappropriately.

The Care & Keeping of You: The Body Book for Girls (American Girl Library)
Valerie Schaefer
A great guide for girls about their bodies and all the changes of puberty—including information about nutrition, sports safety, feelings, and how to insert a tampon. It's one of several wonderful American Girl Library social issue books.

The Girls Body Book: Everything You Need to Know for Growing Up YOU!
Kelli Dunham
This book, for girls only, is a smarter version of The Care & Keeping of You. Helpful comments from real girls, as well as inspirational quotes throughout, help make this one a winner.

The Boy's Body Book: Everything You Need to Know for Growing Up YOU!
Kelli Dunham and Steven Bjorkman
The go-to guide for boys about their bodies and the changes of puberty, this book discusses skin, hair, family relationships, friendships, and wet dreams. This book offers advice and support for boys only.

For ages 10 and older

It's Perfectly Normal! Changing Bodies, Growing Up, Sex and Sexual Health
Robie Harris and Michael Emberley
The older kids' version of Robie Harris's other book, this book is for kids 10 and older. It covers puberty, masturbation, sex, sexuality, same sex relationships, birth control, STIs and HIV, pregnancy, birth, and healthy relationships. It contains a lot of information and detail in a simple, easy-to-read package.

What's Happening to Me? A Guide to Puberty
Peter Mayle
This book, for kids 10 and older, talks about the changes of puberty for boys and girls. The truly funny illustrations make this a fun and informative read.

The "What's Happening to My Body?" Book for Girls
—A Growing Up Guide for Preteen and Teens
Lynda Madaras with Area Madaras
This book includes many details about the changes of puberty, information about sex, sexual feelings, birth control , and STIs and HIV.

What's Going on Down There? Answers to Questions Boys Find Hard to Ask
Karen Gravelle with Nick and Chava Castro
This thoughtful book for boys explains in detail the changes of puberty, sex and sexual feelings, masturbation, birth control, and STIs and HIV. It includes interviews with men, reflecting on their own experience of puberty.

For ages 14 and older

Changing Bodies—Changing Lives
Ruth Bell and others
Written by the authors of Our Bodies, Ourselves, this book is for teens 14 and older and covers everything—and I mean everything about sex and sexuality. It includes tons of testimonials on every topic by real teens.

Body Drama—Real Girls, Real Bodies, Real Issues, Real Answers
Nancy Redd
I love this book. Written by a former Miss Virginia and Harvard graduate, it's a great book for girls. It presents information in a lively, readable fashion and includes many photographs so girls can see what's normal. Nancy Redd rocks!

What Hollywood Won't Tell you About Sex, Love and Dating
Greg Johnson and Susie Shellenberger
A great book for teens from a Christian perspective. Greg and Susie offer sound advice for waiting to have sex, saying no, dating, and being clear about your values.

RECOMMENDED READING FOR ADULTS

So Sexy, So Soon
—The New Sexualized Childhood and What Parents Can Do to Protect Their Kids
Diane E. Levin, PH. D and Jean Kilbourne, Ed.D.
This book is a must read for every parent. Go get it from the library. Now.

The Talk: What Your Kids Need to Hear from You About Sex
Sharon Maxwell, Ph.D.
Short and to the point, Dr. Maxwell's book covers how our hyper-sexualized world is impacting children's sexuality, how to manage the internet and TV, the importance of sexual desire and the power of sex.

Everything You Never Wanted Your Kids to Know about Sex (But Were Afraid They'd Ask):
The Secrets to Surviving Your Child's Sexual Development from Birth to the Teens
Justin Richardson and Mark Schuster
My all-time favorite book for parents; these guys know their stuff. It's very readable, funny and full of good ideas and stories about talking to kids about sex. This book will help make the conversations easier.

Sex and Sensibility: The Thinking Parent's Guide to Talking Sense about Sex
Deborah Roffman
A bit denser and tougher to read than my all-time favorite, Roffman's book offers sound ideas for parents to help you prepare for and tackle this important part of parenting.

Protecting the Gift, Keeping Children and Teenagers Safe (and Parents Sane)
Gavin De Becker
This is a wonderful book that explains the importance of helping our kids be savvy when they are out in the world. It's sometimes disturbing, but De Becker knows his stuff and really helps parents learn how to keep kids safe.

Smut: A Sex Industry Insider (and Concerned Father) Says Enough is Enough
Gil Reavill
This dad tells the tale of pornography and its impact on our kids, families, and culture. He knows what he's talking about—he worked in the industry as a writer.

Pornified: How Pornography is Damaging Our Lives, Our Relationships, and Our Families
Pamela Paul
The title says it all.

The Primal Teen
—What the New Discoveries about the Teenage Brain Tell Us about Our Kids
Barbara Strauch
This book explains what is going on inside that crazy teen brain. Strauch explains neurology and how the brain works in a concise, fairly easy to read book.

Positive Discipline A-Z: 1001 Solutions to Everyday Parenting Problems
Jane Nelsen, Lynn Lott, and Stephen Glenn
The definitive guide to parenting from the heart, this book will help your kids behave better and you become a better parent.

ONLINE RESOURCES

Child Sexual Abuse

StopItNow.org—Stop It Now!
ChildMolestationPrevention.org—The Child Molestation Research and Prevention Institute
POMWA.org—P.E.A.C.E. of Mind—*Non-scary and pragmatic tips for keeping kids safe.*

How to talk to kids about sex and general sexuality information

AdvocatesForYouth.org—Advocates for Youth - *includes information for gay kids.*
NoPlaceLikeHome.org—No Place Like Home for Sex Education—*a great year-by-year guide.*
SIECUS.org—The Sexuality Information and Education Council of the United States
TeenPregnancy.org—National Campaign to Prevent Teen and Unwanted Pregnancy
ASHASTD.org—The American Social Health Association—*STI information.*

Internet safety

Zoo.com—Kid-safe browser.
NetSmartz.org—National Center for Missing and Exploited Children
WebWiseKids.org—Web Wise Kids. *Includes an excellent game called "Missing."*
IKeepSafe.org—Internet Keep Safe Coalition. *Games and activities for younger kids and parents.*
GetNetWise.org—Internet Education Foundation. *Reviews of safety products for your computer.*

Pornography

ThePornTalk.com—*Really good, detailed information for talking to kids about pornography.*
MediaFamily.org—National Institute on Media and the Family. *Talking to kids about pornography—the short version.*

Other online resources

BirdsandBeesandKids.com—Birds + Bees + Kids® *My website for ordering resources, scheduling talks, professional trainings, workshops, and one-on-one consultations.*
MySistahs.org—*For young women of color.*
YouthResource.com—Advocates for Youth. *Information for gay, lesbian, transgendered or questioning youth.*

REFERENCES

Albert, B. (2007),
With One Voice: America's Adults and Teens Sound Off About Teen Pregnancy.
Washington, DC: National Campaign to Prevent Teen Pregnancy.

Advocates for Youth,
Abstinence-Only-Until-Marriage Programs: Ineffective, Unethical, and Poor Public Health,
http://www.advocatesforyouth.org/publications/policybrief/pbabonly.htm
Accessed August, 22, 2008.

Laura Duberstein Lindberg, Ph.D. and others,
Non-coital Sexual Activities Among Adolescents,
The Guttmacher Institute, December 2007.

Advocates for Youth,
Young People and HIV,
http://www.advocatesforyouth.org/publications/factsheet/fshivaid.html
Accessed October 17, 2008.

Center for Disease Control,
HIV/AIDS Among Youth,
http://www.cdc.gov/hiv/resources/factsheets/youth.htmHIV
Accessed September 6, 2008.

Advocates for Youth,
Abstinence-Only-Until-Marriage Programs: Ineffective, Unethical, and Poor Public Health,
http://www.advocatesforyouth.org/publications/policybrief/pbabonly.html
Accessed October 17, 2008.

Kaiser Family Foundation,
Sex on TV4,
http://www.kff.org/entmedia/upload/Sex-on-TV-4-Full-Report.pdf
Accessed October 17, 2008.

Guttmacher Institute,
Facts on Induced Abortion in the United States,
http://www.guttmacher.org/pubs/fb_induced_abortion.html
Accessed January 1, 2009.

In addition to teaching what to say and when, how to keep kids safe, and tips and tricks to make the conversations more effective, Amy Lang, MA provides parents and caregivers with an environment that encourages them to explore their personal values about sexuality, love, and relationships. Her goal is to help parents decide what is right for their family based on their values. She also works with professionals to help them learn about natural and healthy childhood sexual behaviors and when to be concerned. She lives in Seattle, has been married for over fifteen years and has a young son who keeps her on her toes playing Legos, digging and asking questions like, "How long do you have to lie like that?" when they talk about how babies are made. Amy is also the author of **The Ask Anything Journal**.